Prayer

Discovering What the Scripture Says

TIMOTHY JONES
& JILL ZOOK-JONES

FISHERMAN
BIBLE STUDY SERIES

PRAYER

PUBLISHED BY WATERBROOK PRESS

12265 Oracle Boulevard, Suite 200

Colorado Springs, CO 80921

ISBN 978-0-87788-709-6

Published in the United States by WaterBrook Multnomah, an imprint of the Crown Publishing Group, a division of Random House Inc., New York.

Printed in the United States of America

2013

18 17 16 15 14 13 12 11

Contents

How to Use This Studyguide v

Introduction 1

1 Praying Like Jesus 3
   Matthew 6:9-13

2 How Shall We Come? 7
   Luke 18:9-14; Hebrews 4:14-16

3 Great Is the Lord! 11
   Psalm 145; 1 Thessalonians 5:16-18

4 A Cry for Forgiveness 15
   1 John 1:8-10; Psalm 51

5 Don't Be Afraid to Ask 19
   James 5:13-18; Luke 11:9-13

6 Prayers for the Kingdom 23
   Ephesians 6:18-20; 1 Timothy 2:1-7

7 Praying That Just Won't Quit 29
   Luke 11:5-8; 18:1-8

8 A Listening Heart 35
   John 10:1-5; 1 Samuel 3:1-21

9   Two Are Better Than One 39
    Matthew 18:19-20; Hebrews 10:23-25

10 When the Door Won't Open 43
    Psalm 13; 2 Corinthians 12:7-10

11 The Arsenal of Prayer 49
    Ephesians 6:10-18

12 When Words Fail Us 53
    1 Corinthians 2:6-16; Romans 8:26-27

Leader's Notes 57

How to Use This Studyguide

F isherman studyguides are based on the inductive approach to Bible study. Inductive study is discovery study; we discover what the Bible says as we ask questions about its content and search for answers. This is quite different from the process in which a teacher *tells* a group *about* the Bible—what it means and what to do about it. In inductive study, God speaks directly to each of us through his Word.

A group functions best when a leader keeps the discussion on target, but the leader is neither the teacher nor the "answer person." A leader's responsibility is to *ask*—not *tell*. The answers come from the text itself as group members examine, discuss, and think together about the passage.

There are four kinds of questions in each study. The first is an *approach question*. Asked and answered before the Bible passage is read, this question breaks the ice and helps you start thinking about the topic of the Bible study. It begins to reveal where thoughts and feelings need to be transformed by Scripture.

Some of the earlier questions in each study are *observation questions*—who, what, where, when, and how—designed to help you learn some basic facts about the passage of Scripture.

Once you know what the Bible says, you need to ask, *What does it mean?* These *interpretation questions* help you discover the writer's basic message.

Next come *application questions,* which ask, *What does it mean to me?* They challenge you to live out the Scripture's life-transforming message.

Fisherman studyguides provide spaces between questions for jotting down responses as well as any related questions you would like to raise in the group. Each group member should have a copy of the studyguide and may take a turn in leading the group.

A group should use any accurate, modern translation of the Bible such as the *New International Version,* the *New American Standard Bible,* the *New Living Translation,* the *New Revised Standard Version,* the *New Jerusalem Bible,* or the *Good News Bible.* (Other translations or paraphrases of the Bible may be referred to when additional help is needed.) Bible commentaries should not be brought to a Bible study because they tend to dampen discussion and keep people from thinking for themselves.

Suggestions for Group Leaders

1. Thoroughly read and study the Bible passage before the meeting. Get a firm grasp on its themes and begin applying its teachings for yourself. Pray that the Holy Spirit will "guide you into all truth" (John 16:13) so that your leadership will guide others.

2. If any of the studyguide's questions seem ambiguous or unnatural to you, rephrase them, feeling free to add others that seem necessary to bring out the meaning of a verse.

3. Begin (and end) the study promptly. Start by asking someone to pray that every participant will both understand the passage and be open to its transforming power. Remember, the Holy Spirit is the teacher, not you!

4. Ask for volunteers to read the passages aloud.

5. As you ask the studyguide's questions in sequence, encourage everyone to participate in the discussion. If some are silent, try gently suggesting, "Let's have an answer from someone who hasn't spoken up yet."

6. If a question comes up that you can't answer, don't be afraid to admit that you're baffled. Assign the topic as a research project for someone to report on next week, or say, "I'll do some studying and let you know what I find out."

7. Keep the discussion moving, but be sure it stays focused. Though a certain number of tangents are inevitable, you'll want to quickly bring the discussion back to the topic at hand. Also, learn to pace the discussion so that you finish the lesson in the time allotted.

8. Don't be afraid of silences; some questions take time to answer, and some people need time to gather courage to speak. If silence persists, rephrase your question, but resist the temptation to answer it yourself.

9. If someone comes up with an answer that is clearly illogical or unbiblical, ask for further clarification: "What verse suggests that to you?"

10. Discourage overuse of cross references. Learn all you can from the passage at hand, while selectively incorporating a few important references suggested in the studyguide.

11. Some questions are marked with a ✐. This indicates that further information is available in the Leader's Notes at the back of the guide.

12. For more information on getting a new Bible study group started and keeping it functioning effectively, read *You Can Start a Bible Study Group* by Gladys M. Hunt and *Pilgrims in Progress: Growing Through Groups* by Jim and Carol Plueddemann. (Both books are available from WaterBrook Press.)

SUGGESTIONS FOR GROUP MEMBERS

1. Learn and apply the following ground rules for effective Bible study. (If new members join the group later, review these guidelines with the whole group.)

2. Remember that your goal is to learn all you can *from the Bible passage being studied.* Let it speak for itself without using Bible commentaries or other Bible passages. There is more than enough in each assigned passage to keep your group productively occupied for one session. Sticking to the passage saves the group from insecurity ("I don't have the right reference books—or the time to read anything else.") and confusion ("Where did *that* come from? I thought we were studying _____.").

3. Avoid the temptation to bring up those fascinating tangents that don't really grow out of the passage you are discussing. If the topic is of common interest, you can bring it up later in informal conversation after the study. Meanwhile, help one another stick to the subject.

4. Encourage one another to participate. People remember best what they discover and verbalize for

themselves. Some people are naturally shy, while others may be afraid of making a mistake. If your discussion is free and friendly and you show real interest in what other group members think and feel, the quieter ones will be more likely to speak up. Remember, the more people involved in a discussion, the richer it will be.

5. Guard yourself from answering too many questions or talking too much. Give others a chance to share their ideas. If you are one who participates easily, discipline yourself by counting to ten before you open your mouth.

6. Make personal, honest applications and commit yourself to letting God's Word change you.

Introduction

Few areas of the Christian life inspire more resolutions— or create more guilt—than prayer. "I know I should pray, and I want to," a friend of ours confesses, "but it's a struggle."

Many of us grapple with not knowing *how* to pray. We long to address God but aren't sure what to say. We want to speak freely, but our prayers fall into stale routines or well-rutted patterns.

We share the longing expressed by one of Jesus' disciples when he exclaimed, "Lord, teach us to pray" (Luke 11:1). Although the disciples had known years of praying, they sensed something different about the way Jesus talked with the Father. They saw a depth and reality in his relationship with God that made them uncomfortable with their dry devotional times and restless for something more. Jesus was happy to show them a better way; his pattern for prayer has become one of the most loved passages of the New Testament.

Scripture is filled with guidance for praying. Its many-splendored teachings and model prayers can enrich your times with God. They can turn your empty resolutions into times of intimacy and fruitfulness. As you begin this study, let your prayer be that of the disciple who came to Jesus, anxious to learn. And let your heart be open to God's Word, for he is eager to teach you to pray.

Praying Like Jesus

MATTHEW 6:9-13

We never get beyond [the Lord's Prayer];
not only is it the Lord's first lesson in praying,
it is all the other lessons, too.
—J. I. PACKER, *I Want to Be a Christian*

Surely the most famous and oft-quoted prayer of the Bible is the one Jesus taught his disciples—the Lord's Prayer.

And with good reason. This is far more than a "rote prayer" to be said woodenly or routinely. Here Jesus introduces the great themes of praying: praise, confession, and petition. He reveals the One we address in prayer and shows us what we can appropriately ask for ourselves.

Since in the Lord's Prayer we're repeating the words and themes Jesus himself taught us, we know we're praying at God's invitation—and according to his will. What better starting place for learning about prayer?

1. When you sit down to pray, how do you begin? How do you know what to include?

READ MATTHEW 6:9-10.

    *2.   To whom does Jesus address this prayer?

    *3.   How can God be both close ("Our Father") and far off ("in heaven")?

    *4.   What kind of response did Jesus expect when he addressed God as his heavenly Father?

    5.   Notice that one of the first phrases in this prayer praises God (*hallowed* means holy, revered). Why is it important to begin our prayers by acknowledging God's greatness?

---

6. What pictures come to mind when you hear the word *kingdom*? Is it here now, coming in the future, or both?

READ MATTHEW 6:11-13.

7. What does Jesus tell us we should ask for ourselves?

8. How do you typically approach God with your needs (examples: confidently, tentatively, humbly)? Explain your answer.

9. Does Jesus' use of imperative verbs (i.e. "give us...forgive us...lead us") mean we should demand that God give us what we need? Why or why not?

10. Which lines in the prayer refer to our relationships with others?

11. Why would Jesus link the forgiveness of our sins with our willingness to forgive other people? How have you seen this confirmed as a principle of life?

12. Jesus tells us to regularly pray for deliverance from evil. What does our need for such a prayer demonstrate about our world and ourselves?

13. When you pray, do you ever fear that God may not be listening? How can knowing we pray in Jesus' own words help us get past our fears and keep on praying?

How Shall We Come?

LUKE 18:9-14; HEBREWS 4:14-16

I cannot imagine any one of you tantalizing your child by
exciting in him a desire that you did not intend to gratify.
It [would be] a very ungenerous thing to offer alms to
the poor, and then when they hold out their hand for it,
to mock their poverty with a denial.… Where God leads
you to pray, He means for you to receive.
—CHARLES SPURGEON, QUOTED IN
Spiritual Disciplines for the Christian Life

As you will soon see, the two Scriptures in this study seem to contradict each other. One suggests we can only approach God humbly. The other instructs us to come confidently. How do the two fit?

It all has to do with perspective. Because of who *we* are, we can never come into God's presence proudly demanding that he do our bidding. We should remember that "all have sinned and fall short of the glory of God" (Romans 3:23). And so we come to prayer depending on his mercy.

But because of who *God* is, we do not shrink back in fear. God's compassion will not allow him to turn a deaf ear to our cries. His love is the ground on which we can confidently stand whenever we approach him.

1. Do you come easily to prayer? When have you needed courage to speak to God?

Read Luke 18:9-14.

2. Jesus had a target audience for this parable. To whom did he address it, and why is this significant?

3. There are two people in Jesus' parable: a Pharisee and a tax collector. What did these titles tell Jesus' listeners about each person?

4. Despite the Pharisee's righteous actions ("I fast twice a week and give a tenth of all I get"), why was God not pleased with him?

5. We sense the tax collector's discomfort at being in the temple. What do you think brought him there?

✐ 6. What does it mean to be "justified before God"?

READ HEBREWS 4:14-16.

✐ 7. Name two things Jesus does as high priest.

8. Because of Jesus, what can we expect to receive from God?

9. How does the invitation to "approach the throne of grace with confidence" fit with the parable's rebuke of the Pharisee's confidence?

10. Psalm 24 admonishes that only he who has "clean hands and a pure heart" should come into God's presence. Have you ever felt that you were not good enough to talk with God? Explain your answer.

11. How can prayer be a time to *receive* something, not just say something? What do you expect God to give you when you sit down to pray?

Great Is the Lord!

PSALM 145; 1 THESSALONIANS 5:16-18

A friend of ours has been cultivating what he calls "an attitude of gratitude." For too long, he believes, his thinking and praying have been laced with discontent. Now he wants to replace his grumbling with a habit of praise.

The Bible has much to say about our friend's new goal. In the New Testament alone, the passages that urge or describe praise and thanksgiving number well over two hundred. And the words themselves take on astonishing variety: *bless, thank, worship, glorify, magnify, extol*—to name just a fraction. Then we uncover the rich vocabulary of praise in the Old Testament. The psalm for this study is a fine example.

Writer Annie Dillard suggests that this approach to prayer grows more significant as we age or face mortality. The dying, she surmises, pray not "please," but "thank you." As we move closer to God's presence, grateful praise saturates our hearts. This "attitude of gratitude" establishes a mature and exciting foundation for our prayer life.

1. Why do you pray? What do you hope to accomplish?

READ PSALM 145:1-2, 21.

2. These verses frame the psalm. Make a list of the
    verbs used in these verses and define them.

3. What is the psalmist praising God for in these
    verses? What does the psalmist's use of extremes
    (*for ever and ever, every,* etc.) teach us about God's
    worthiness and our responsibility?

READ PSALM 145:3-7.

4. What is it about God that makes him worthy of
    praise?

5. Again, note the verbs *(commend, tell, proclaim).*
    How can our praises serve to teach our children
    about God?

✐ 6. What are some of God's "mighty acts" and "awesome works" that we can commend to our children?

7. Verse 7 speaks of celebrating God's goodness and
singing of his righteousness. How can this verse help
us incorporate praise into our worship services?

READ PSALM 145:8-20.

8. Name some of the characteristics of God for which
we might praise him.

9. According to verses 11 and 12, praise has a role in
evangelism. What might that be?

READ 1 THESSALONIANS 5:16-18.

✐ 10. Do you experience constant joy in your life? If so, where does it come from? If not, do you find this admonition a simple reminder to count your blessings, or an unrealistic and burdensome expectation?

✐ 11. Think over the schedule of an average day in your life. Where could you fit prayer and thanksgiving into your day?

12. Why do being joyful, praying continually, and giving thanks in all circumstances fit together into God's will for us? How can prayer, especially thankful prayer, make us joyful?

A Cry for Forgiveness

1 JOHN 1:8-10; PSALM 51

We once knew a woman whose husband had grown sullen and distant. Communication had ground to a standstill. As if the emotional barrenness of her home were not enough, our friend began to question whether God still accepted her. She confessed, "I'm afraid that because I find it hard to want to work on my marriage, God won't hear my prayer. I feel unworthy, and it's driving me farther from God, not closer."

We talked about the radical truth of the Christian faith: We don't have to have perfect lives in order to approach God in prayer. His stubborn, forgiving love—not our goodness—determines the outcome of our praying.

We can count on the fact that in our fallenness we will sometimes fail. Can we depend just as certainly on God's promise to forgive?

1. How did you feel as a child when you realized you had done something your parents wouldn't like? Have you ever experienced that feeling as an adult?

READ 1 JOHN 1:8-10.

   2. How do you understand this passage in the light of Jesus' words in Matthew 5:48: "Be perfect, therefore, as your heavenly Father is perfect"?

   3. If we say we do not sin, we actually do two things. What are they?

   4. What happens when we confess our sins? How can this knowledge free you when you approach God's throne in prayer?

READ PSALM 51:1-6.

   5. What characteristics of God make confession inviting?

6. What must occur in us before we are willing to confess?

7. When we do something to injure or upset another person, why would we confess that to God? According to verse 4, against whom have we actually sinned?

⌀ 8. What did Jesus' death and resurrection accomplish for us in our dilemma of being "sinful at birth"?

READ PSALM 51:7-12.

⌀ 9. Note the anxiety expressed here by the sinner. What does unconfessed sin do to our relationship with God?

10. Sin made the psalmist feel unclean. How does he describe the experience of forgiveness for which he longs? If you can, describe a time you felt this way after prayer.

READ PSALM 51:13-19.

11. For the psalmist, forgiveness brings an eager desire to tell people about God. Discuss how our experience of sin and consequent forgiveness can bring others to Christ.

12. Have you made confession a regular part of your prayer time? What would be the value in doing so?

Don't Be Afraid To Ask

JAMES 5:13-18; LUKE 11:9-13

P rayer is sometimes just a matter of asking. "Often it is the simple, repetitious phrases that our Father in heaven finds most irresistible," said seventh-century writer John Climacus. "One phrase on the lips of the tax collector was enough to win God's mercy; one humble request made with faith was enough to save the good thief."

Prayer need not be something we fear we won't get "just right." In fact, Jesus reminded his followers that "your Father knows what you need before you ask him" (Matthew 6:8). Scripture teaches us that God delights to hear us—always. He offers us a standing invitation. "Come, all you who are thirsty," he said through his prophet Isaiah (55:1). "Ask...seek... knock," said Jesus to his disciples (Matthew 7:8). "In everything," said Paul the apostle, "present your requests to God" (Philippians 4:6).

1. What happens when you must accept a gift from another person? Do you feel obligated to "return the favor"?

READ JAMES 5:13-18.

2. According to these verses, when should we pray?

3. What is a "prayer offered in faith"?

✐ 4. Why was Jesus' prayer in Gethsemene (Mark 14:36; Luke 22:42) a "prayer offered in faith"? How can you pray with this kind of faith in your own circumstances?

5. Do these verses suggest that God's answers to our prayers are limited by our righteousness (verse 16) or our earnestness (verse 17)? Consider Luke 17:6 as you explain your answer.

6. Note the promises in verses 15 and 16: Prayer "will make the sick person well"; "he will be forgiven"; pray so that "you may be healed." On what are these promises based?

✍7. Who is "a righteous man," and how well does this phrase describe you? What could make your prayers more "powerful and effective"?

Read Luke 11:9-13.

✍8. List each verb along with the result Jesus says it will produce.

9. Can we take verse 10 literally? If we ask God for something—anything—will we get it, or will we find limits to God's generosity?

10. Who do you think Jesus means when he says "every-one" (verse 10)? Does he mean "every person," or "everyone who is a disciple," or "everyone who comes in faith," or something else?

⚲ 11. What does Jesus mean when he says, "knock and the door will be opened to you"? Consider verse 13. What is Jesus urging us to seek?

12. Do you sometimes feel self-centered in asking God for what you personally need? Do you try to lay your own concerns aside when you pray for fear they may be trivial? Consider this quote from C. S. Lewis and try to put it into practice this week:

> We must lay before [God] what is in us, not what ought to be in us.... It may be that the desire can be laid before God only as a sin to be repented; but one of the best ways of learning this is to lay it before God.... If we lay all the cards on the table, God will help us to moderate the excesses....Those who have not learned to ask Him for childish things will have less readi-ness to ask Him for great ones. (C. S. Lewis, *Letters to Malcolm, Chiefly on Prayer*)

Prayers for the Kingdom

EPHESIANS 6:18-20; 1 TIMOTHY 2:1-7

*For years it has been my practice in traveling among the
nations to make a study of spiritual movements which
are doing most to revitalize and transform individuals
and communities. At times it has been difficult to
discover the hidden spring, but invariably.... I have
found it in an intercessory prayer life of great reality.*
—MISSIONARY JOHN R. MOTT

One of the privileges of prayer is to intercede for the
advancement of God's kingdom in the world. In intercession we take people, specific situations, our churches—even
whole nations—to God. We invite him to intervene and carry
out his will. This may mean praying for missionaries carrying
the gospel to the far corners of the earth or praying for a min-
istry to the homeless in our own community.

We sometimes forget how significant such praying can be.
"More things are wrought by prayer than the world dreams
of," wrote the poet Alfred Tennyson.

Jesus had such praying in mind when he urged us to pray
"thy kingdom come." The writer of Psalm 67 had it in mind

when he prayed, "that your ways may be known on earth, your salvation among all nations." And in this study the apostle Paul tells us even more about the importance of prayer for the kingdom's advance.

1. When you're reading the newspaper or watching the news on TV, do you ever feel moved to pray for someone mentioned there? If so, share some specific examples and how you prayed.

READ EPHESIANS 6:18-20.

2. What does Paul mean when he tells us to "pray in the Spirit"?

3. Name all the kinds of prayer you can think of. How can we use the many varieties of prayer to make certain we "pray...on all occasions"?

4. Paul urges his readers to "be alert" in their praying, and instructs them to "always keep on praying." Why does he seem so urgent?

5. Paul tells us to pray "for all the saints." *Saint* is one of the New Testament's favorite words for *believers.* Using verses 19-20, how can you pray for pastors, missionaries, people in your church, and other Christians?

6. What specific way did Paul want the Ephesians to pray for him? Verse 20 discloses that Paul is writing from prison—why did he not ask them to pray for his release?

7. Who do you know whose prayer request might be similar to Paul's—"that I may declare [the gospel] fearlessly, as I should"? In what part of your daily schedule can you plan to spend time praying for him or her?

READ I TIMOTHY 2:I-7.

8. To whom does the "everyone" in verse 1 refer? What do prayers have to do with "all men" being saved (verse 4)?

9. Verse 2 singles out "kings and all those in authority" as an important focus for our intercession. What is the promised outcome of our prayers for those in authority?

10. Does it make you uncomfortable to pray for governmental leaders, especially those with whom you disagree? Do you think that prayer for our nation's leaders should be a regular part of church worship services? Why or why not?

11.   How might verses 3-6 guide us as we pray for missionaries and the spread of the gospel throughout the world?

12.   Besides prayers for the world's spiritual needs, how can we touch the physical world in our requests, our intercessions, and our thanksgiving? Write three sentence prayers that lift to God the world's needs.

13.   If you've concluded from this study that you need to give more attention to intercession, in what specific ways can you do so? Can you describe any areas in which to intercede besides the ones mentioned in this study?

Praying That Just Won't Quit

LUKE 11:5-8; 18:1-8

*The great fault of the children of God is they
do not continue in prayer; they do not go
on praying; they do not persevere. If they
desire anything for God's glory, they
should pray until they get it.*
—GEORGE MÜLLER

Nineteenth-century Christian writer George Müller was not implying that prayer is a blank check whereby we demand that God perform according to every wish or whim. Instead, he was underlining the fact that sometimes we give up too easily.

That's an especially important lesson for our culture of instant gratification. We are unused to persisting.

Jesus told a parable that suggests that we may sometimes be polite or lazy to the point of indifference in our praying. Here we learn to keep approaching the Father—even when the answer won't come easily.

1. Tell about someone in your life—a parent, teacher, child, salesman—who refused to give up in his or her efforts to convince you to be or do something.

READ LUKE 11:5-8.

2. Note that the man in Jesus' parable went to a friend, someone with whom he had already established a relationship. How might the story have been different if he had approached a stranger?

3. What did the man in the parable ask his friend? Was it a reasonable request, made under reasonable circumstances? Explain.

4. Notice that in Jesus' time the man could not simply run out to an all-night grocery store or take his guest to a restaurant. How did his need give energy to his request? When in your life has desperation pushed you to keep asking for something?

5. At first the friend refused to help the man. What made him change his mind?

6. Some versions of the Bible read, "because of the man's *persistence*" in verse 8. Others read, *"boldness."* Discuss the passage from the differing perspectives of these two words.

READ LUKE 18:1-5.

7. What was the character of the judge in the parable? Why did he at first refuse to give the widow a just settlement?

8. What caused the judge to change his mind? Did his character change?

READ LUKE 18:6-8.

9. Jesus both compares God to the unjust judge and contrasts their characters. How did Jesus say God and the judge were alike? How are they different, and why does this bring us such hope?

10. How does persistent prayer differ from the "bab-bling" of the pagans, who "think they will be heard because of their many words" (Matthew 6:7)? If God knows what we need before we ask him (Matthew 6:8), why should we "cry out to him day and night" (Luke 18:7)?

11. Jesus closes this lesson on prayer with an unsettling question: "When the Son of Man comes, will he find faith on the earth?" How would you answer Jesus?

12. Have you ever stayed up all night praying for an-other person or a particular concern? How does the idea of persistent, persevering prayer fit with the common adage, "Let go and let God"?

A Listening Heart

JOHN 10:1-5; 1 SAMUEL 3:1-21

*The moment you wake up each morning, all
your wishes and hopes for the day rush at you
like wild animals. And the first job each
morning consists in shoving it all back;
in listening to that other voice, taking that
other point of view, letting that other, larger,
stronger, quieter voice come flowing in.*
—C. S. LEWIS

In our desire to include many people and situations in our praying, we may forget that prayer is more than talking. Faithful praying often has a leisurely sense of quiet. We may "accomplish" much in our praying by simply waiting in the Lord's presence for his comfort, insight, or guiding word.

Despite our hurried, harried lifestyle, Psalm 46:10 reminds us to pause long enough to consider the Lord: "Be still, and know that I am God." You see, fruitful prayer relies not just on an active mind or busy tongue, but on a quiet heart that listens for God.

1. Tell about a time when you needed to know God's will concerning a decision facing you. How did you attempt to discover it? Do you feel that you ever did?

Read John 10:1-5.

2. How does the shepherd in this parable lead his sheep?

3. The watchman (verse 3) apparently oversees an area where several flocks are penned. Which sheep does the shepherd call to follow him when he comes into the pen?

4. How are the sheep able to recognize the shepherd's voice (see John 10:14)? What do they do when they hear the voice of a stranger?

5. Jesus likens himself to the shepherd (see John 10:11). Who, then, do the sheep represent?

6. In what ways does Jesus "call" or speak to us? How can we tell his voice from that of a "stranger" who would pretend to be him or call us to follow other leaders in different directions?

Read 1 Samuel 3:1-21.

7. How does the writer of 1 Samuel describe the times during which the boy Samuel lived?

8. Notice how long it took Eli to recognize that it was God who called Samuel. In what way might his slowness be related to the description of the times in verse 1? What part might his own sinfulness play?

9. Why did Samuel not recognize God's voice? What role did Eli play in Samuel's life at this point?

10. Note that God did not relay his message until Samuel showed himself ready to listen. What might that suggest to us about our prayers? How can silence—a receptive, listening silence—become an appropriate part of prayer in your life?

11. What is the significance of verse 18? Would Samuel have trusted his vision without Eli's confirmation?

12. How do today's times compare with those described in verse 1? How does God communicate with us today? What is our part in listening and responding?

Two Are Better Than One

MATTHEW 18:19-20; HEBREWS 10:23-25

A soul which remains alone is like a burning coal which is left by itself: It will grow colder rather than hotter," said sixteenth-century spiritual writer John of the Cross. Centuries before, the writer of Ecclesiastes observed, "Two are better than one… If one falls down, his friend can help him up. But pity the man who falls and has no one to help him up!… Also, if two lie down together, they will keep warm. But how can one keep warm alone?" (Ecclesiastes 4:9-11).

All of us need others to help us stay spiritually warm. Prayer has an individual aspect, to be sure, but it is never merely private. We may pray in our closet, but we also need to pray with others. Only then will our misconceptions experience testing, our spirits find new strength, and our prayers grow to maturity.

1. Describe a time when the stress or confusion of a situation caused you to seek another person with whom to pray.

Read Matthew 18:19-20.

✐ 2.　To whom does Jesus refer when he says "two of you" in verse 19?

✐ 3.　What does Jesus promise will happen "if two of you…agree about anything you ask for"?

✐ 4.　How do you interpret such a sweeping promise? If we pray with another for something, does this guarantee we will get it?

5.　What does Jesus say will happen when "two or three" gather in his name?

6. What is the significance of Jesus being present? How does that affect our prayer times together?

7. If you pray regularly with another person or with a group, what benefits have you discovered? If you have not practiced this kind of prayer, who might you trust to share times with God?

Read Hebrews 10:23-25.

8. How might we use a prayer time with other Christians to "spur one another on toward love and good deeds"?

9. The Greek word translated "give up" in verse 25 refers to desertion and abandonment. When we "abandon" meeting with one another, what do we lose?

10. One poll showed that 70 percent of Americans say they have many acquaintances, but few close friends, and that this causes a void in their lives. When have you experienced loneliness in your Christian life? How could praying with one another offer an antidote to our loneliness?

11. What might "meeting together" encompass? Name settings and occasions besides Sunday morning worship that you have found particularly encouraging. Have these included prayer?

If you can, try calling a friend or a person you respect about a particular need you have this week. Ask him or her not only to pray for you during the week, but to pray with you over the phone. If you don't feel comfortable on the telephone, try to meet your friend somewhere with the sole purpose of praying together.

When the Door Won't Open

PSALM 13; 2 CORINTHIANS 12:7-10

have lived to thank God that all my prayers have not been answered," said one writer whose perspective helps us understand those times when God doesn't appear to be listening.

Many of us recall situations when what *seemed* so necessary or urgent turned out not to matter. Or we found that the object of our request might have hurt us. We may long for power that would ruin us, for a relationship that would drain us, for a job that would not suit us. God takes the long view, and in his mercy he may say no.

Unanswered prayers can also teach us about waiting, God's dependable care in times of hardship, our own need to develop character, or the necessity of persistence and spiritual warfare. However, some unanswered requests remain a mystery. For all our praying, waiting, and believing, God sometimes will not answer a prayer that by all our accounts looks good.

The Bible amazingly reassures us that in an important sense there is no such thing as unanswered prayer. God may not answer as we expect or want, but he always listens and always responds.

1. Recount an incident when you prayed earnestly for something and God seemed not to answer.

READ PSALM 13.

2. According to the psalmist, why had God not answered his previous prayers?

✍ 3. Does the psalmist seem faithless to you when he accuses God of forgetting him and delaying response to his prayers? What does it mean to cry out to God?

4. As we've seen in a previous study, Jesus urged persistence in praying. But what motivates such persistence? What is the role of unanswered prayer in teaching us perseverance?

5. Quickly outline the psalm, noting the progression of the thoughts expressed by the psalmist. How did the very act of praying bring him relief?

Read 2 Corinthians 12:7-10.

6. Paul suggests an interesting reason why God might allow suffering. What is it? When and how has God dealt with you in a similar way?

7. Three times Paul "pleaded with the Lord" to take away the "thorn." What made him willing to plead? Why did he stop pleading after the third time?

8. Paul's prayer did not go unanswered. God simply said no. What did God's answer help Paul understand about himself?

9. Is there such a thing as unanswered prayer? How can we tell when God is answering our prayer with a *no*?

10. How is God's power made perfect in weakness? How have you seen this in your life or in the life of someone you know?

11. Tell about a time in your life when God's answer to your prayer seemed delayed. What do you now see as a purpose to God's answering with a *wait*?

12. According to the models provided by both the psalmist and Paul, there is at least one faithful conclusion to be drawn from an experience of "unanswered" prayer. What is it?

13. What does a child learn about God when his or her earnest prayer for a bike goes unanswered? How can God use what we perceive to be unanswered prayer to teach us about himself?

The Arsenal of Prayer

EPHESIANS 6:10-18

To hear some believers talk about the Christian life, you might imagine it's simply a pleasant stroll.

The apostle Paul, in contrast, described it as a battle. He used warfare imagery and spoke of standing ground under the assault of spiritual evil.

Prayer, then, is not always gentleness and peace. Sometimes it feels like a gritty struggle. "The church at large," writes Michael Green in *Exposing the Prince of Darkness*, "seems to have lost the recognition that there is a war on. 'Church' is a place to go on a Sunday once a week—or month—not a corps of battle troops under a commander against a skillful, powerful, ruthless foe."

Here Paul teaches us how to be soldiers for Christ. He trains us to employ the armor of God, as we find strength for the battle in him.

1. Have you ever experienced a time when praying required an intense struggle? What was the nature of the struggle?

READ EPHESIANS 6:10-18.

2. In these verses Paul writes about "our struggle"—
   about our need to "be strong in the Lord" and "to
   stand." What does this suggest about the Christian
   life?

 3. Against whom do we struggle, according to Paul?
    What examples can you give of this kind of
    struggle?

4. If our struggles are not against "flesh and blood,"
   how do we develop discernment to see past the
   human face of evil to the dark power that motivates it?

5. Paul makes it clear that human strength is not sufficient to fight this battle. Mere physical armor cannot protect us nor give us the victory. Why?

6. What are the various pieces of the "armor of God" that Paul urges us to don? How does each piece protect us or equip us?

7. What part does prayer play in this spiritual warfare? How do we battle in prayer for someone?

8. One way we stand our ground against evil is to keep ourselves pure and righteous. Paul writes, "You were once darkness, but now you are light in the Lord. Live as children of light" (Ephesians 5:8). How can prayer help us to set "the breastplate of righteousness in place" (6:14)?

9. How do we take up the "shield of faith" (verse 16)? How can prayer strengthen our faith?

✐ 10. Look again at each piece of God's armor. Pray sentence prayers for a specific way you need God to strengthen and protect you in each area.

When Words Fail Us

1 CORINTHIANS 2:6-16; ROMANS 8:26-27

W hen one of our sons was a toddler, recurring ear infections dulled his hearing and slowed his mastery of speech. But that didn't stop him from joining in our nightly family prayer times. When his turn came, he "prayed" in what can only be described as an unrolling string of unintelligible syllables with all the inflection and rhythm of real language. He was earnest, but didn't have the words.

Sometimes words are hard in coming for our adult prayers too. We may not know what to say. We may find words insufficient to articulate all that is within. Our speech may seem a poor vehicle for communication in the presence of an awesome God.

The Bible gives us good news for such times. The Holy Spirit himself, whom Paul says "searches all things, even the deep things of God," comes to help us in our praying. That means we never pray alone or unaided.

1. Name times in your life when words have seemed inadequate to express your feelings.

READ 1 CORINTHIANS 2:6-16.

2. Paul speaks of God's "secret wisdom" that no one has seen nor heard nor even thought of. How, then, do we know about it?

3. Who knows God's thoughts (verse 11)? How does Paul conclude we can know God's thoughts (verse 12)?

4. What is the nature of the "spirit of the world" (verse 12)? How does that spirit affect a person's ability to understand the things of God (verse 14)?

5. What does "the Spirit who is from God" do for us?

6. Paul recognized that the message he preached came to him from the Spirit, in words specifically given by the Spirit. How does this concept relate to our prayer life?

READ ROMANS 8:26-27.

7. What "weakness" is Paul referring to here?

8. How does the Spirit help us in our weakness?

9. In the previous passage Paul wrote about the words that the Spirit gives us. Here he writes about "groans that words cannot express." What does he mean? How is human language too limited (too *human*) to express all that the Spirit wants us to pray? What options do we have?

10. Do you turn away in frustration from prayer when you can't seem to find the words? Have you ever asked the Holy Spirit to intercede for you? If so, what was the result?

11.   Have you ever awakened from a sound sleep sensing
       that you needed to pray for someone? How do you
       think the Holy Spirit was involved in this? What
       happened?

12.   Sometimes we can feel such a longing to express
       something to God, but the longing doesn't seem
       easily put into words. Do we have to use words in
       order to pray? Why or why not?

13.   Think back over the weeks you have been studying
       prayer. How has your prayer life improved? How
       can you further work on your communication with
       God?

Leader's Notes

STUDY 1: PRAYING LIKE JESUS

Question 2. When we begin with "Our Father," we do so at nothing less than Jesus' invitation. We are God's children by adoption through the person and work of Jesus (see John 1:12-13 and Ephesians 1:3-6). Because of Jesus, we approach God as confident children, expecting a ready and compassionate response.

Question 3. Herein lies the hope of the Lord's Prayer: the One who loves us with the care and compassion we would expect from a perfect Father is also the one "who is able to do immeasurably more than all we ask or imagine" (Ephesians 3:20).

Question 4. See Luke 11:11-13, where Jesus portrays God as a loving Father.

Question 10. When we received Christ, God adopted us as his children (John 1:12-13). But we are not alone as we look to him as Father. We have many brothers and sisters in Christ. Thus we pray *our* Father, not *my* Father. In an important sense, this is a prayer for Christians to pray together. It contains elements important for our life together in the church ("forgive us our debts, as we also have forgiven our debtors").

Question 12. "Christians cannot disregard evil around and within them, nor are they at liberty to try, for their calling is to face evil and overcome it with good (Romans 12:21). But this assumes that evil does not overcome them....The moment we cry 'deliver,' God's rescue operation will start; help will be on the way to cope with whatever form of evil threatens us" (J. I. Packer, *I Want to Be a Christian*. Wheaton, IL: Tyndale House Publishers, 1979).

STUDY 2: HOW SHALL WE COME?

Question 3. The Pharisees were an influential sect within Judaism. While we think of them as rigid, envious, and formulistic (see Mark 2:16), Jesus' hearers would have thought of them as godly. Tax collectors, on the other hand, had a terrible reputation. They were Jews, but they collected taxes for the Roman government. They sometimes defrauded the people and were often despised by their countrymen.

Question 4. Consider the Pharisee's focus. He addressed his prayer to God, but he focused not on God's greatness or goodness, but on his own behavior. "All our righteous acts," wrote Isaiah, "are like filthy rags" outside of a humble relationship with God (Isaiah 64:6). "For it is by grace you have been saved, through faith—and this not from yourselves, it is the gift of God—not by works, so that no one can boast" (Ephesians 2:8-9).

Question 6. According to the dictionary, one who is justified is shown to be just or right, free from blame, guiltless. God finds guilt-free those who have faith in Jesus, for "all have sinned and fall short of the glory of God, and are justified freely by his grace through the redemption that came by Christ Jesus" (Romans 3:23-24; see also verses 25-28).

Question 7. The following Scriptures shed light on what Jesus does as "high priest" and how his priesthood differs from that of the Old Testament and Jewish priests: Hebrews 5:1-10; 7:23-25; 9:24-28; 10:11-22. In these, we find Christ both a mediator between God and humans and a sacrifice for our sins.

Question 9. There is a great difference between *confidence* and *pride*. With pride, we approach others—and God—as if we were superior or extraordinary. When we are proud, we focus on *self*. On the other hand, we approach God in confidence when we come depending on his goodness and mercy.

Question 10. If you find people in your group who are sincerely wrestling with feeling "good enough" to talk with God, be sure to extend empathy, reassurance, and prayer. Stress the core of this study: None of us is righteous—we're only able to come near to God because of his overwhelming mercy toward us.

STUDY 3: GREAT IS THE LORD!

Question 3. We often think of praise in terms of what God does. These verses praise him for who he *is*.

Question 6. You can find lists of God's accomplishments, beginning with Creation, in several of the psalms. Of course we can add to these lists his great work in Jesus Christ and our personal experiences of his power.

Question 10. A number of verses in the New Testament urge us to pray with thanksgiving, especially Ephesians 5:19-20.

Question 11. Consider thanking God for food as you wash the dishes, for an able mind as you enter data into your computer at work, for the dependability of creation as morning follows night again. Pray for your child's growing relationship with God as you remove his bicycle from the middle of the driveway. Look for other ways to bring God into every moment of your day.

STUDY 4: A CRY FOR FORGIVENESS

Question 2. Some commentators argue that the word *perfect* in Matthew 5:48 suggests completeness or maturity. Does this shed a new and somewhat relieving light on the passage?

Question 4. Think back to Hebrews 4:14-16. Knowing that our sins have been forgiven helps us to come to God boldly with our requests and praise. We need not fear his wrath because Jesus has taken the punishment for us, and therefore God sees us as pure and eligible to approach him.

Question 8. Paul addresses this question at some length in Romans 5:12-19, where he contrasts Adam, who introduced sin and death into the world, with Christ, who brought righteousness and life.

Question 9. One major consequence of unconfessed sin is alienation from God. We may have trouble feeling close to God. Often we feel our spiritual life stagnating, as if we are just "going through the motions," and that brings us immense dissatisfaction. And when our relationship with God is ailing, other parts of our lives follow suit. See also Psalm 32:1-4 and Isaiah 59:1-2.

Question 11. Forgiveness brings new joy and a fresh awareness of God's mercy. We are eager to tell people about this wonderful God and to praise him in their hearing. The psalmist emphasizes not his sin, but the Righteous One who saved him.

Question 12. The Book of Common Prayer has a key phrase in its prayer of confession that can help us understand the value of confessing our sins to God: "Father, we confess.... Have mercy on us and forgive us, *that we may delight in your will and walk in your ways to the glory of your name.*"

Study 5: Don't Be Afraid to Ask

Question 4. Jesus knew "that in all things God works for the good of those who love him, who have been called according to his purpose" (Romans 8:28). Believing that God's plans are perfect, compassionate, and just, Jesus submitted his will to God's.

Question 7. James 5:17 speaks of Elijah as a "man just like us" who "prayed earnestly" to great effect. Remember that God considers us righteous by virtue of our belief in Christ Jesus (Romans 3:22). Then, even if our faith is as small as the smallest seed (Luke 17:6), God can accomplish his plans through us. The more time we spend in prayer, the more opportunities we give God to work through our prayers.

Question 8. Jesus' perspective might prove difficult for the passive or weak-kneed. Note with what aggressive verbs he admonishes us to pray. In the original language of the New Testament, the verbs "ask...seek...knock" literally mean, "*keep* on asking...*keep* on seeking...*keep* on knocking."

Question 11. You can prod answers to this question a little further by asking, "Where is the door and how do we knock on it? Who will open the door?" Other passages that will shed light on these verses are Matthew 6:33, John 14:26, and John 16:13-14.

Study 6: Prayers for the Kingdom

Question 2. The Living Bible paraphrases this "in line with the Holy Spirit's wishes." Check various translations to find what other meanings this phrase could have.

Question 4. Look back at Ephesians 6:11-13. We'll study more about the desperate battle we fight in study 11.

Question 7. If you can, take time at the end of the study to pray for those people mentioned here.

Question 9. See Jeremiah 29:7, where peace and prosperity for God's people depends upon the peace and prosperity of the city.

Question 10. This brings up an interesting question: How do we pray for those in authority when they persecute believers? The Roman emperor Nero—a notorious persecutor—ruled when Paul wrote these words. Because Nero "needed a scapegoat for the great fire that destroyed much of Rome in A.D. 64…he blamed the Roman Christians. Persecution erupted throughout the Roman Empire. Not only were Christians denied certain privileges in society, some were even publicly butchered, burned, or fed to animals. Social ostracism was

widespread" (*Life Application Bible,* Wheaton, IL: Tyndale
House Publishers, Inc., 1988, p. 1864).

Study 7: Praying That Just Won't Quit

Question 7. Widows in biblical times were in a particularly vul-
nerable situation. An uncaring judge could ignore their requests. With the widow in Jesus' parable, persistence—not her
social standing—eventually compelled the judge to bring her
justice.

Question 10. The pagans counted upon the effectiveness—
almost the magic effect—of the words themselves. Instead, we
must come to prayer depending on the response of an accessi-
ble and loving God.

Question 11. You may wish to restate Jesus' question as follows:
When Christ comes again in the end times, will he find any
who, standing "firm to the end" (Matthew 24:13), persevere in
faith and prayer?

Question 12. Note these two occasions from the life of Jesus
where persistent, sustained prayer preceded important junc-
tures: Luke 6:12-13; 22:39-46.

Study 8: A Listening Heart

Question 5. A common image for God in the Old Testament
was that of Shepherd. Psalm 23, Isaiah 40:11, and Jeremiah
31:10 all suggest that God shows people the kind, competent
care of a loving shepherd. Consider how this imagery and

background would have affected Jesus' hearers when he applied the image to himself.

Question 8. See 1 Samuel 2:29-31. During the rule of Israel's judges, which represented the period just prior to that described in 1 Samuel, we hear of only two prophets (Judges 4:4; 6:8). This helps explain the comment in 1 Samuel 3:1 that "in those days the word of the Lord was rare."

Question 9. Although Samuel was no longer a child (1 Samuel 2:21, 26), he was still quite young. He had never heard God's voice for himself and was not familiar with its sound. He needed a more mature believer to help him learn to listen.

Question 11. If time allows, discuss how mature spiritual leaders may help us in our own processing of what God reveals to us.

Study 9: Two Are Better Than One

Question 2. See Matthew 18:1.

Question 3. This is not the only place Jesus demonstrated his belief in the "power of two." See Luke 10:1, where we read of Jesus sending out the seventy-two disciples, "two by two ahead of him to every town and place where he was about to go."

Question 4. Note that even Jesus prayed with an attitude of submission to the Father's will: "Yet not my will, but yours be done," he prayed in Gethsemane (Luke 22:42). While our prayers are always answered according to God's will, Jesus implies here that we may receive more answers when we pray together.

Question 9. Somehow, meeting together with other people spurs us on toward spiritual growth. Notice that even though Jesus didn't necessarily agree with all that was happening among the religious leaders, he still did not abandon meeting at the temple and synagogues. Stories of his times in God's house are sprinkled throughout the Gospels.

STUDY 10: WHEN THE DOOR WON'T OPEN

Question 3. Today, people often doubt the reality of God when he does not quickly respond to their requests. The psalmist never questions God's existence. Rather, his is the voice of faith, crying out to the One on whom he depends.

Question 5. Consider this simple outline:

Verse 1: The psalmist questions God's failure to respond to previous prayers.

Verse 2: He anxiously evaluates his situation.

Verses 3-4: He recognizes that God alone can bring relief to him.

Verses 5-6: He remembers God's goodness to him in the past. That memory revitalizes his hope and inspires his praise, calming his anxiety and lifting his spirit.

Question 7. A "plea" is the heartfelt, often anguished cry for aid to someone who is superior to us. Making such a plea can be a humiliating experience, one that reminds us of our weakness and dependence. Evidently, God's message to him (2 Corinthians 12:9) was so strongly communicated that Paul was satisfied with it—he didn't feel God hadn't answered him, but that he had answered with a no.

Question 8. "Not all of our prayers produce the results we want. Even after years of waiting, the answer to a legitimate request may be no. God is not our errand boy. He can't be manipulated by our formulas, bargains, or tears.... Is God wise, good, merciful, powerful, loving, faithful, and gracious? If so, then he can be trusted with a no. He doesn't owe me an explanation. Faith is being certain of what I do not see. If I could see why God was saying no to my request, I would be living by sight, not by faith" (Martha Reapsome, *The Journey of a Lifetime,* Wheaton, IL: Harold Shaw Publishers, 1993, pp. 77-78, 80).

STUDY 11: THE ARSENAL OF PRAYER

Question 3. Paul also mentions powerful beings in the unseen realm in Ephesians 3:10.

Question 5. "These evil rulers, satanic beings, and evil princes of darkness are not people, but fallen angels over whom Satan has control. They are not mere fantasies—they are real. We face a powerful army whose goal is to defeat Christ's church" (*Life Application Bible,* p. 1817).

Question 10. Leave plenty of time for this question! If you can, pair off into partners so that those in your group can pray for each other to be strengthened in their weaker areas.

STUDY 12: WHEN WORDS FAIL US

Question 2. The "secret," or mystery, was once hidden, but was revealed and made clear with the resurrection of Christ. These passages use similar terminology: Romans 16:25-26; Ephesians 3:4-5; and 1 Timothy 3:16.

Question 3. We learn God's will in several ways: through the Bible, for example, or through what others tell us. But a very important aspect in recognizing God's will is listening intuitively to his Spirit. What makes our hearts leap—or our "danger signals" flash? After we pray about a given situation, what answer brings us peace? These are signs of the Holy Spirit speaking to us, warning us, or reassuring us. Talk with your group about other indications of God communicating his will.

Question 4. See also John 8:42-47.

Question 6. "It is not necessary that we should always know; indeed, perhaps we shall never fully know what any of our prayers wholly mean; God's answer is always larger than our petition, and even when our prayer is most definite and intelligent there is a wide margin which only the Holy Ghost can interpret, and God will fill it up in His infinite wisdom and love" (A. B. Simpson, quoted in *World Shapers,* compiled by Vinita Hampton and Carol Plueddemann. Wheaton, IL: Harold Shaw Publishers, 1991, pp. 48-49).

In addition to the resources previously referred to in this book on the topic of prayer, also see Richard Foster's *Prayer* (Harper San Francisco, 1992).

The Fisherman Bible Studyguide Series—
Get Hooked on Studying God's Word

Old Testament Studies

Genesis

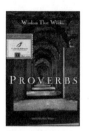

Proverbs

New Testament Studies

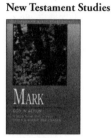

Mark

John

Acts 1-12

Acts 13-28

Romans

Philippians

Colossians

James

1, 2, 3 John

Revelation

Women of the Word

Becoming Women of Purpose

Wisdom for Today's Woman

Women Like Us

Women Who Believed God

For more information, visit our Web site: www.waterbrookmultnomah.com

Topical Studies

Building Your House on the Lord

Discipleship

Encouraging Others

The Fruit of the Spirit

Growing Through Life's Challenges

Guidance and God's Will

Higher Ground

Lifestyle Priorities

The Parables of Jesus

Parenting with Purpose and Grace

Prayer

Proverbs & Parables

The Sermon on the Mount

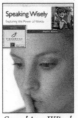

Speaking Wisely

Spiritual Disciplines

Spiritual Gifts

Spiritual Warfare

The Ten Commandments

When Faith Is All You Have

Who Is the Holy Spirit?